More Vintage Halloween

A Grayscale Adult Coloring Book
48 Vintage Coloring Pages

Grayscale Coloring Books

Vicki Becker

Copyright © 2017 Vicki Becker.
All rights reserved worldwide.

About the Author

Vicki Becker is an avid needlework enthusiast who loves everything arts and crafts! Mrs. Becker has been knitting and crocheting for over 48 years. She learned to crochet from her grandmother in the beautiful Adirondack Mountains of upstate New York where she grew up.

Mrs. Becker shares her knowledge and experience through her books with patterns for crochet, knitting, hand embroidery, and quilting. Vicki also enjoys making puzzle books, journals, and coloring books. She creates digital art, illustrations, and mixed media art for the designs in her books.

Vicki Becker lives in central Florida with her husband, four cats, and two dogs. Her hobbies include all forms of needlework, photography, digital art, cooking, and gardening.

What Is Grayscale Coloring?

Grayscale coloring means that you will be coloring over a black-and-white picture. The magic of coloring over grayscale is that the shading is already done for you! Even beginners with no knowledge of shading can achieve beautiful results. Colored pencils work beautifully with the grayscale images giving the finished picture depth and dimension. The paper is well suited for colored pencils but does not work as well with markers. If you use markers put a sheet of paper under the page in case of bleed-through.

Copyright © 2017 Vicki Becker. All rights reserved worldwide.

No part of this publication may be replicated, redistributed, or given away in any form or by any means, including scanning, photocopying, or otherwise without the prior written consent of the copyright holder.

The vintage images in this book are copyrighted in their present, altered format. The images were compiled and developed to create a grayscale coloring book.

ISBN-13: 978-1977914880

ISBN-10: 1977914888

First Printing, 2017
Printed in the United States of America

Hallowe'en Greetings.

Colorists Name

Date

A FARM PRODUCT

Halloween Greetings.

At the witching hour hang a bell of Gold Round a cats neck and he'll do what he's told

Hallowe'en

Hallowe'en Secrets

The wise old owl, who works at night,
Knows lucky secrets good and bright.
Consult him at the witching hour,
'Twill bring you joy and wealthy dower.

Colorists Name

Date

HALLOWE'EN PRECAUTIONS.

If at midnight with a pumpkin light
You steal to your room unseen
In the mirror appears the face,
Of your lover true, on Hallowe'en

Colorists Name

Date

Colorists Name

Date

A THRILLING HALLOWE'EN

Ye GHOST

Wishing you a Highly Entertaining HALLOWEEN

Colorists Name

Date

HALLOWE'EN GREETINGS

I'm not afraid of any witch
That wields the meanest
  kind of switch
Or owls that hoot a
  mournful sound
When elves like you
  are hovering
    round

Colorists Name

Date

Colorists Name

Date

Colorists Name

Date

Colorists Name

Date

Colorists Name

Date

Colorists Name

Date

Colorists Name

Date

Colorists Name

Date

Colorists Name

Date

Colorists Name

Date

Colorists Name

Date

Colorists Name

Date

Colorists Name

Date

Colorists Name

Date

Colorists Name

Date

Colorists Name

Date

Colorists Name

Date

'TIS HALLOWEEN TONIGHT
AND ALL PRETTY GIRLS ARE WITCHES BEWARE

Colorists Name

Date

A Happy Halloween

The Clock is striking Midnight,
The Witch her Spell will cast,
All the Fairies, Ghosts   Goblins,
Will be conjured   ast.

Made in the USA
San Bernardino, CA
12 December 2017